BOOK 1

Christmas Kaleidoscope

8 New Arrangements of Traditional Carols
for the Intermediate to Late Intermediate Pianist

• •

Martha Mier

Each Christmas season brings to us a colorful kaleidoscope of beautiful sights and sounds. Music fills the air! Traditional Christmas carols spread the message of love, peace and joy as we celebrate this very special season with friends and loved ones.

Just as a kaleidoscope constantly changes in colors and patterns, the solos in *Christmas Kaleidoscope* offers a variety of styles. Discover a surprise in the baroque styling of "Deck the Halls," or enjoy the quiet, gentle lullabies for the Christ Child in the beautiful melodies of "Joseph, Dearest Joseph" or "Lullay, Thou Little Tiny Child." The spirit of joyous celebration rings out in "Carol of the Bells" and "I Heard the Bells on Christmas Day."

Begin your newest musical adventure now, and discover the beauty and excitement that shines through these special arrangements in *Christmas Kaleidoscope!*

Merry Christmas!

Contents

Alfred

Copyright © MCMXCXI by Alfred Music
All rights reserved. Produced in USA.

Cover photo: © Ken Reid/FPG International Corp.
Music engraving: Nancy Butler

D1416126

Away in a Manger

Traditional German Carol
Arr. by Martha Mier

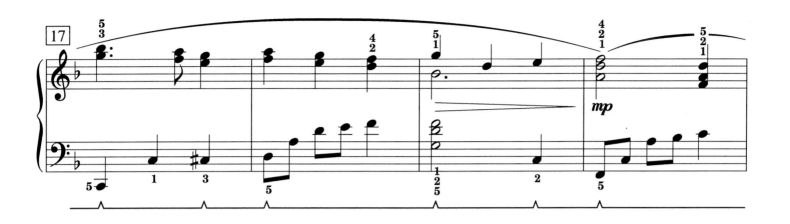

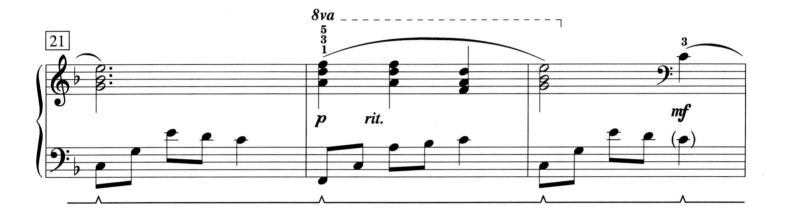

Carol of the Bells

M. Leontovich
Arr. by Martha Mier

Joyfully, fast

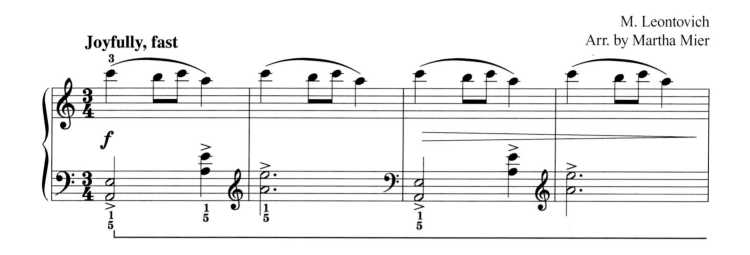

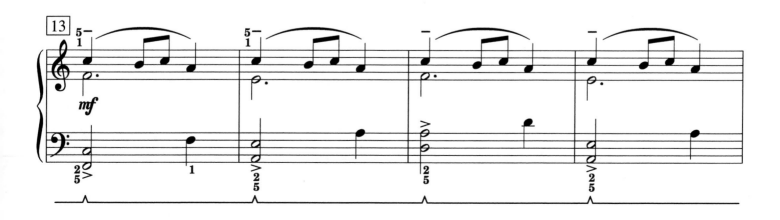

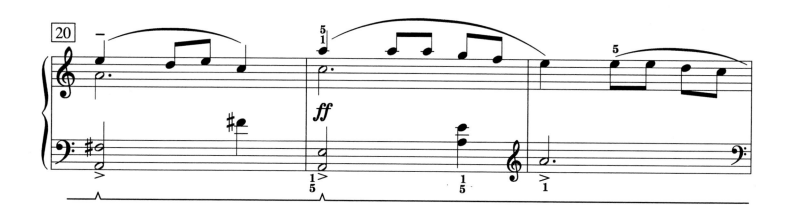

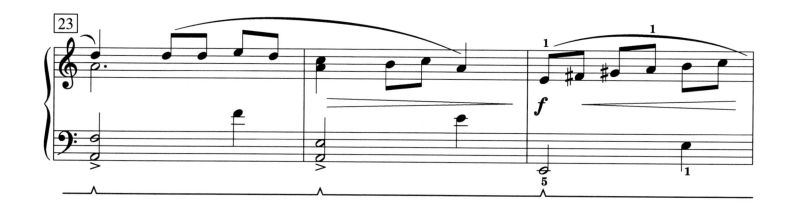

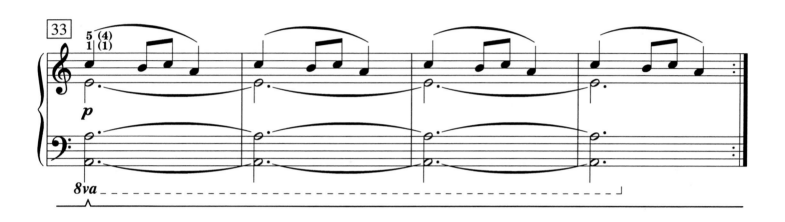

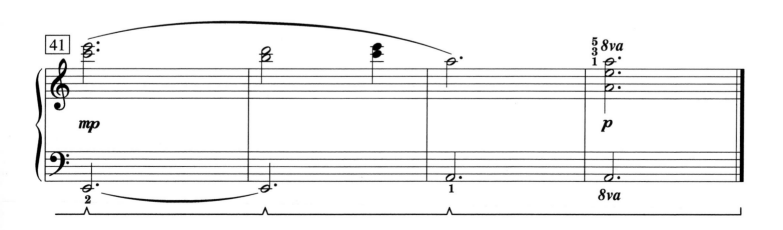

The Holly and the Ivy

Traditional French Carol
Arr. by Martha Mier

What Child Is This?

With simple tenderness

Old English Melody
Arr. by Martha Mier

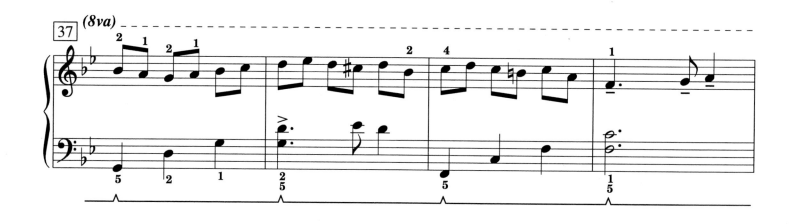

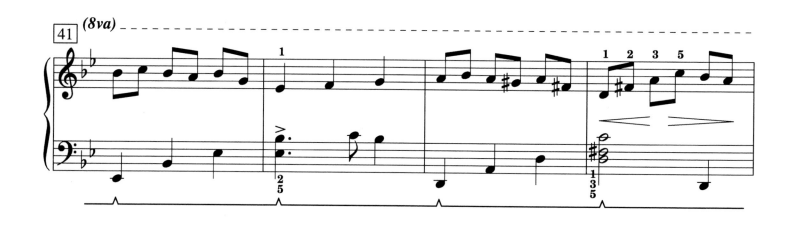

I Heard the Bells on Christmas Day

J. Baptiste Calkin
Arr. by Martha Mier

Joseph, Dearest Joseph

Traditional German Carol
Arr. by Martha Mier

Quietly, peacefully

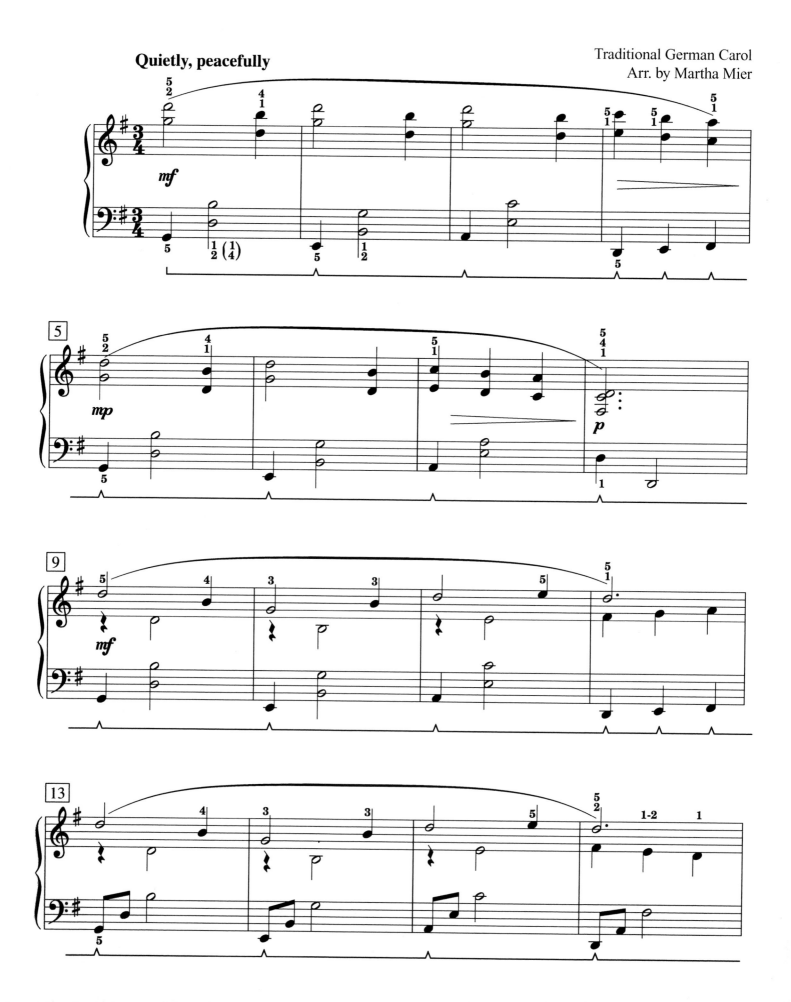

Lullay, Thou Little Tiny Child
(The Coventry Carol)

Traditional English Melody
Arr. by Martha Mier

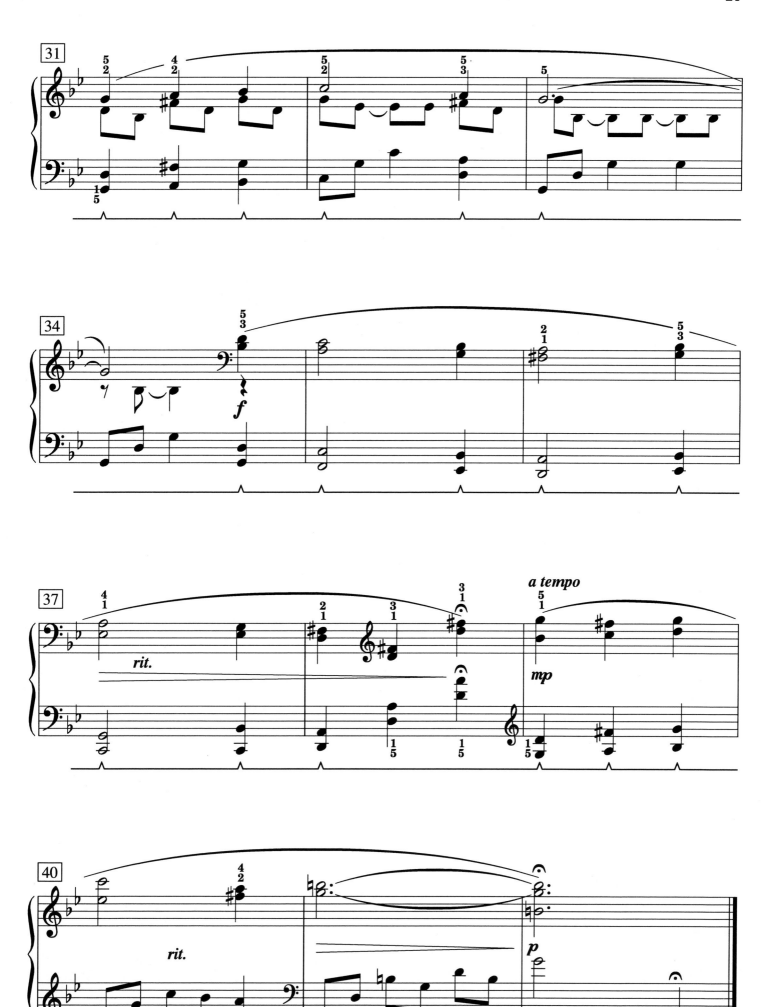

Deck the Halls

Traditional Welsh Carol
Arr. by Martha Mier

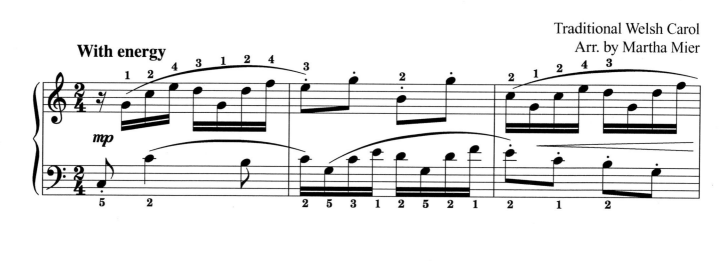

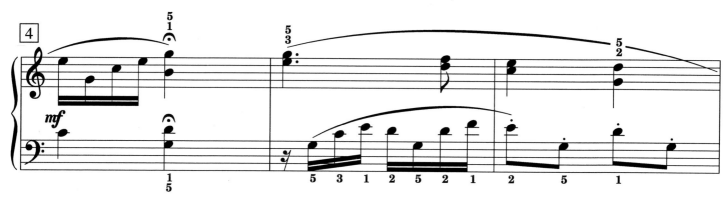

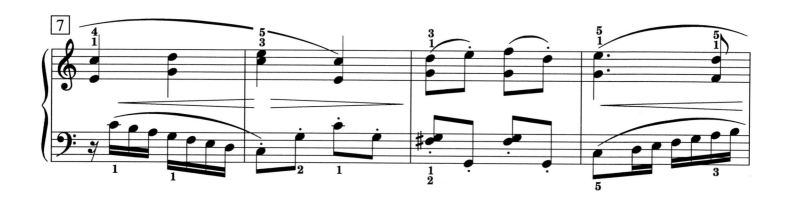

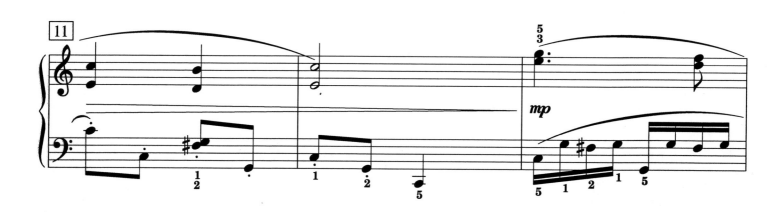

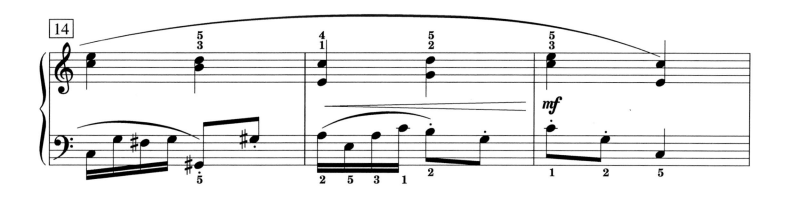

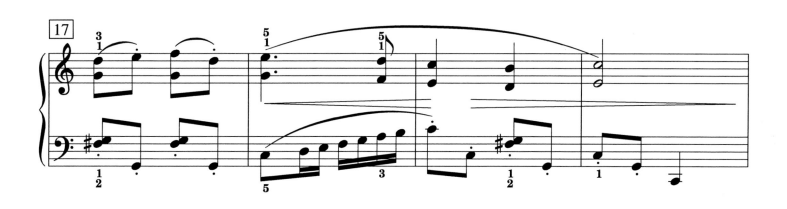

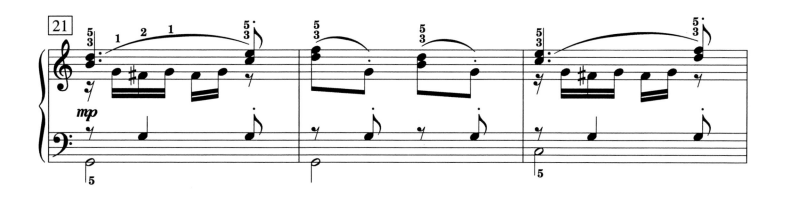

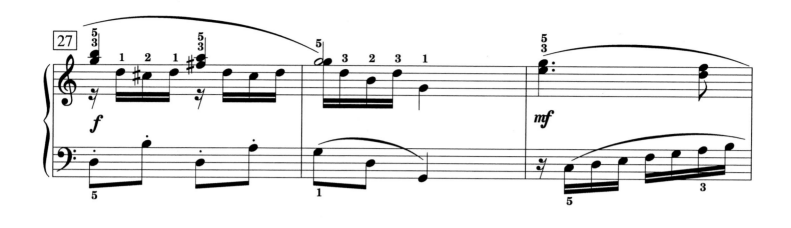

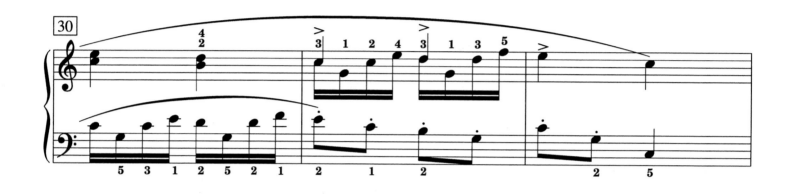